Tales from Dada's Farm

Dedication

This book is dedicated to all the farmers, gardeners, and nature lovers of the world. To everyone who loves to grow plants.

To all the gentle folks who encourage kindness to animals and see them as living creatures who can experience happiness as well as pain.

To the people who cherish moral values such as honesty and truthfulness and don't think these are uncool.

To all who are considerate of all other fellow humans.

Table of Content

Dana and Daria Visit Grandpa

Spring had arrived and it was glorious out in the farm. The daffodils and the daisies had started to peep through the plush-green meadow. Buds were beginning to flower, adding a splash of color and birdsong echoed through the trees. Flowers were everywhere, and everything was alive.

It was Dana and Daria's first visit to the farm. Grandpa was thrilled to see them both. To welcome them he had baked Blueberry cream cake, their favorite treat. Dada was an adventurous baker and he loved to make treats for the kids. For this cake, he had woken up early to pick the blueberries that had started to ripen in the greenhouse and got fresh goat milk from the barn.

After a snack of warm milk and cake, he took them on a short hike through the farm. They stopped to say hello to Soni the goat in the barn who was soaking up the sun with her brood of baby goats. Daria discovered to her delight that the haystack next to the barn could serve as a wonderful trampoline. She had hours of fun climbing and jumping on the haystack, while Dana made a watercolor of the farmhouse which had a charming old dug well with an iron bucket on the pulley.

an old fashioned well
at Dada's farmhouse
with a
bucket & pulley

Now it was evening, and Dana was ensconced in his camp cot behind the mosquito curtain. In the calm, perfectly still night the monotonous mosquito music jarred on restless Dana.

When one enterprising beastie found its way in through a tiny hole in the net, and bit into Dana's smooth forehead, Dana made a mad swap for the savage bug. The little mosquito however escaped and started buzzing around.

Dana knew that insects such as bumblebees act as plant pollinators, yet he could not help feeling infuriated with the bugs that were biting him.

as nature awakens
in glorious spring,
the insects
come out too!

Dana was feeling unhappy, and the bloodthirsty bugs added to his agitation.

"You are such a fine boy," Dana's grandpa had remarked," but you have been very quiet today. I hope you are well."

How perceptive grandpa was, Dana thought, since he was being kept awake by a far more disturbing thought than the droning hum of the snow mosquitos. He finally pulled the blanket over his chill shoulders with a firm resolve that tomorrow morning he would sneak out with his backpack and return to his home.

Ever since arriving on the farm, his shy smile had won him grandpa's instant adoration, but deep in his boy heart, that little voice continually mocked him with "Liar, liar."

"I can't imagine how I shall explain things to mama, that's what is bothering me most. I wish I hadn't done it. Why was I such a fool? I thought I was getting some easy money, but I have been feeling so sick inside."

There were soft footsteps on the path outside his room, and then Dana heard voices. It was grandpa and the new farmhand, Aman. He could see them plainly now through the window, and — he rose to his elbow anxiously—they had found the empty wallet! Was he hearing straight? How could that possibly be? Hadn't he lobbed it far out in the fishpond near the farmhand's cottage?

"Found it," he exhaled. "Oh, what a fool! I might have known someone would find it, and yet no one goes out to that abandoned fishpond. Why didn't I hide it somewhere else?" thought Dana.

The two men passed Dana's room on their way to the barn, and he could hear them talking in low voices.

"My niece couldn't do it, Dada, that's all there is to it," said the farmhand. "I've brought up Sidra since she was a toddler; she is very truthful. She simply could not do it. It would be unfair to accuse Sidra wrongly."

"It must have been someone on the farm," said Grandpa with a frustrated voice. "It simply must have been. And I saw Sidra coming out of my room where she had no business to be. She told me she was trying to find the washroom. It makes me very worried to know that there is a thief on the farm."

Dana slept fitfully and woke up much before dawn with the first crowing of the rooster. He quickly gathered a few of his clothes and stuffed them in his backpack. Slipping out softly, he made for the unpaved track which led to the bus terminal.

The shimmering morning stars peeped down at Dana as he walked on the clumpy, mossy mattress covering the dirt track. He wondered if Daria and his grandpa would miss him. Suddenly, he realized that his mother would be astonished at his unannounced return and the suspicion of theft may also fall on him. He stopped, agonized over his choices, and then turned back toward farm. Slowly he retraced his steps till he came to wooded area which passed near the farmhand's cottage. Haggard and lonely, Dana sat down on a trees stump shifting his bundle on the ground in front of him.

A dozen times he removed the wad of cash from his backpack and looked at them. He had been thrilled that this money would let him buy a new bike. How he now despised the banknotes. Once he had thrown them from him in revulsion, only to collect them carefully again. In front of him lay the swampy fishpond which was home to the wetland creatures such as bull frogs, beavers, and the red fox.

"Why, that's odd," thought Dana "There is a boat floating in the pond with no one in it."

"What's that voice? Cried Dana in sudden alarm. A faint girlish cry of "Help help..." came through the woods. Dana jumped up and was off at a fast start towards the back of the tree clump. "I am coming," he shouted, while panting for breath. In a few moments he emerged from the thicket and sprinted to the shore.

Twenty feet from the shore Dana saw Sidra thrashing frantically in the water gasping for air. She looked scared and was flailing her arms in terror. Dana took in the whole situation quickly. He realized that by the time he went and got help, it might be too late for Sidra.

Dana was not a good swimmer but there was a strong tree branch which overhung the boat. He thought he had a chance of dropping on the boat if could swing on the branch.

In a moment he was scrambling up the tree like a squirrel chased by a cat, bellowing at Sidra to not worry. Now on the tree branch he looked down on the boat, and fear clutched at his throat. What if he missed the boat and fell in the water himself?

Cautiously Dana slid to the end of the branch, and with his heart in his mouth, he let go his grip and struck water. It was just as well that he had missed the boat. He could have destabilized the boat or hurt himself by falling from the tree branch directly into the boat's hard wooden floor.

Dana had missed the boat, but the gunwale was easy to get to. He caught it easily by stretching his hand, lifted himself aboard and then grasping the oars, he rowed to where Sidra was floundering in the water. He was afraid that the boat would run over Sidra if he pointed straight to her, so he carefully circled around her and positioned the boat within easy reach.

As Sidra grabbed the edge of the boat, it tilted over, and water rushed into the boat. Just as it was on the verge of capsizing, Dana hurled himself to the other side of the boat and screamed at Sidra to hold fast to the opposite gunwale and try to come aboard very slowly to avoid pitching the boat.

Sidra was much composed now that she had the boat to hold onto and she clambered aboard, shivering uncontrollably from the cold water. Even as Dana gave her his jacket to wrap herself in, he spied that a bunch of people including Sidra's uncle Aman, and his grandpa dada had arrived on the shore attracted by all the screaming and shouting.

As the exhausted Sidra was carried off the boat by Aman, she picturesquely described how Dana had saved her from drowning without sparing a thought for his own safety.

Dana's mind was full of conflicting emotions. While everybody was applauding his bravery and quick-thinking, a little voice in his mind continued to remind him that he was a thief and a liar. He had stolen the money from his grandpa and let suspicion fall on an innocent girl.

His beloved grandpa was so proud of him and praised him, yet Dana's conscience told him that he was morally bankrupt. He couldn't understand what had possessed him to take something that did not belong to him.

In the evening just as Dana and Daria were finishing evening tea with grandpa, they saw the farmhand, Aman, coming up the stairs with his niece Sidra.

Sidra shyly put out her hand and thanked Dana. She ruefully explained that she had wanted to surprise Dana and Daria with some fresh pike patties for their breakfast, and that's how she happened to be out on the water so early in the morning.

Dana managed to mumble something and hurried back to his room where he sat down with his head in his hands feeling dizzy. He needed to think. If ever he was going to square himself with his conscience it had to be now. He thought it through - it's always hard to tell the truth but he knew that there would not be a better chance than tonight.

As he made his way back to the living room, he could hear the happy chatter of many people grouped around the fireplace. The farmhand, Aman, was saying that Dana was the nicest boy he had known, and he was entitled to a special reward. Tomorrow, he would take Dana to the bike shop and buy him the best bike that Dana would choose.

Daria noticed Dana coming in and she called out to him to come and join them. Dana however stopped near the door and called out to his grandpa. "Grandpa, I am not entitled to the reward that Aman has so kindly offered."

Dana falteringly explained how he had stolen the money and how this act had continued to prey on his conscience. He held out the wad of bills to his grandpa and said with trembling lips, "I am sorry grandpa, I yielded to the temptation. It looked so easy. And I am sorry that I let suspicion fall on Sidra."

A deep silence settled on the flabbergasted group. But his grandpa didn't look angry! He was smiling and held out his hands to Dana. As Dana ran sobbing to his grandpa's embrace, he heard the farmhand say from behind, "Dana, it takes more courage to do what you did just now than to save my niece's life. You have earned not only my lifelong gratitude but also my respect for your truthfulness. I won't insist on giving you the bike as a gift, but I will give you something better. You can teach Sidra how to paint and draw that you do so well. We will sell these paintings in the nearby farmer's market, and perhaps you will make enough money to buy an old bike if not a new and shiny one."

Grandpa said that he needed a temporary farmhand to pick the late spring blueberries and he could let Dana work and earn some more money. He said, "Dana, I didn't know it was possible for me to love you more than what I already did. But now I know. Today my grandson has made me truly proud and happy."

Daria came and hugged her brother. He brother was her idol, and her eyes were shining with happiness at his integrity and bravery.

Dana felt drained as he laid down to sleep that night, but he was content and happy. The droning buzz of the bugs outside his mosquito net no longer bothered him and he drifted off to a peaceful sleep.

Daria Climbs the Magnificent Oak

Daria loved the giant oak tree next to the barn with its magnificent branches soaring to the sky. It had some low branches which made it easy for climbing. One afternoon, Daria took her lunch and climbed up to the top. Navigating through a maze of leafy branches she discovered a comfortable perch on the bough of the tree, and soon settled down to enjoy her chicken sandwich.

Dana had gone over to visit Sidra and now they were both coming back when they saw Daria nestled among the leaves. Sidra gave a scream of joy and clambered up the tree to join her friend.

Daria and Sidra whooped as they scampered up and down the low-hanging branches laughing wildly. They finally climbed down and joined Dana who had brought out his sketch book and was busy laying out the drawing tools on a small makeshift table. He had promised Sidra's uncle, the farmhand, that he would teach her to draw and paint and he created a three-step drawing of the oak tree for Sidra to practice.

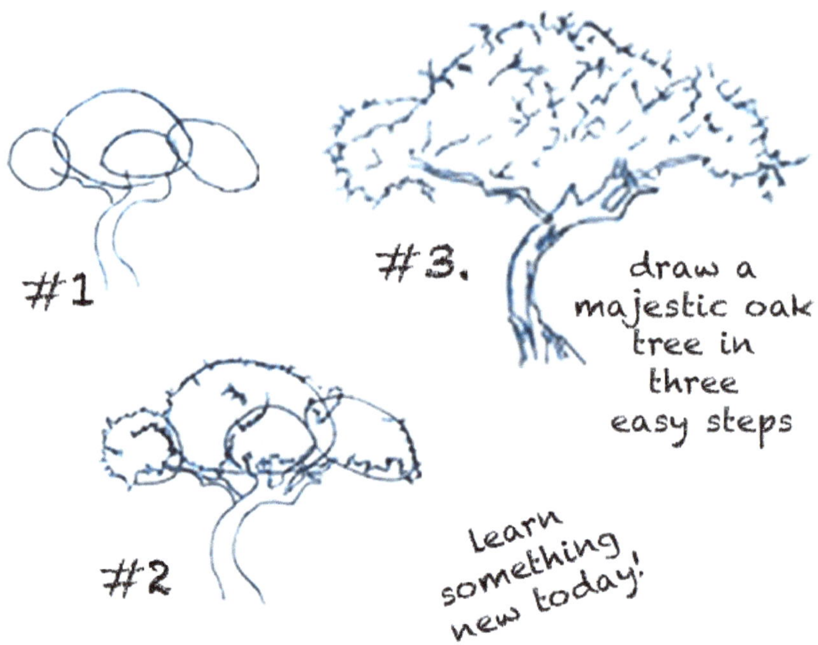

It was a beautiful lazy afternoon and soon grandpa joined the little gang which was busy drawing and painting under the oak tree's shade. The children petitioned him for a story, and he agreed.

"Well, my kids," grandpa said, "I am happy to see you having fun at the farm. This mighty black oak tree is my favorite too. It puts on its thick covering of leaves from year-to-year acts as such a nice and natural umbrella protecting us from the burning glare."

"Yes, grandpa," said Dana, "but I so wish the oak tree had fruits like the peach tree near Sidra's house."

"Here's the oak fruit," said grandpa with a smile.

"But it's just an acorn," exclaimed the astonished kids in unison, "and it tastes so bitter."

"Yes, but what is an acorn if not the fruit of the oak tree?" asked grandpa. They are bitter because they contain a substance called tannin which makes the acorns bitter and unsafe for human beings. But my cows love them, and they seek them out, even though eating a lot of it gives them indigestion.

The acorn is a special favorite among many of the wild creatures such as the deer, gray squirrels, rabbits, and wild turkey. To make it safe for us humans, we need to a boil it with a special processing to leach out the tannin."

"The acorn is such a pretty subject for painting," observed Dana, who had an artists' love for nature. "See Sidra, it has a little green teacup with an exquisitely carved saucer to hold it. These would be great as cups on your doll's tea-table. I once read that in the old days people believed that fairies used the acorns at their feasts."

Sidra smiled shyly as she took the acorn from Dana, and grandpa continued to explain. "The oak tree is certainly associated with a lot of legends Dana. Since it is so tall and moisture rich, it is more often struck by lightning than any other tree. The ancient druids as such believed that oak trees are the sacred sanctuaries of Thor, the mythical thunder-god."

"Yes, grandpa," said Dana, "I read that the ancient druids would stand below the oak tree during thunder, as they believed that they would get transformed into powerful shamans if lightning struck them. They held that lightning has the power of spiritual illumination."

"I would suggest staying away from the oak tree in a thunderstorm Dana," admonished grandpa gently.

"I remember reading about oak apples also grandpa," said Daria. "Are they also fruits of the oak like the acorn?"

"No Daria. Though they are larger than acorns, sometimes as large as an apple, the oak apples, or galls as they are called, are in fact tree barks which have swelled up. Sometimes a wasp would pierce the bark and leaves its eggs in the hole which eventually causes the bark to swell up in a round shape. In the ancient times, romans used the oak apples to make ink as it has a reddish color."

"You said the oak tree is moisture rich, grandpa, could you drill a hole to get sap from oak like we do from the maple trees?" asked Sidra.

"I love how you are so inquisitive about nature Sidra. And yes, all trees produce sap, even so, oak sap is nutty and bitter, and not very palatable."

"I remember grandpa, that each summer, grandma would collect the oak tree bark and dry them in the sun. She would then grind them into powder with her pestle and mortar. Our family used this powder as tea for sore throat or as paste for soothing itchy skins when the bugs bit us." Sidra said.

"Yes, Sidra," grandpa smiled. "Your grandma was an avid herbalist who knew the many ways nature can be our friend. Did you know that the oak tree bark has many other uses? For example, the leather shoes you are wearing have been prepared using a process called tanning for which oak tree barks are used."

When the kids looked astonished, grandpa explained, "I had mentioned that the acorns contain tannin. This tannin is also present in the tree bark, and it has the property of giving consistency and toughness to animal skins and makes the last longer. The animal skins are soaked in water saturated with bark powder for several days, and so the hides become leather."

"Can we make tea from this bark, dada?" Daria playfully had picked up a fallen piece of dried bark and showed it to grandpa.

"No, Daria," said grandpa. "This is the outer bark which has fallen down. The bark used in making herbal medicine is the inner bark which is made up of living tree cells."

"We must be careful, only to remove a very small branch if we collect bark from a living tree," continued grandpa. "Once removed, tree bark does not grow back, and the tree needs the bark as much as we need our skin. The inner bark transports food from the leaves all the way to the roots. The outer bark acts as a waterproof jacket and protects the inner delicate parts of the trunk from temperature changes and invasion of insects. The bark also prevents the evaporation of water as it is being carried up from the roots through the trunk."

"Are there many varieties of oak trees, grandpa?" Dana wonderingly asked.

"Oh, yes; the red dye comes from the bark of the red oak which is very common in America. The cork oak grows in Europe and Africa, and its bark is used to make the cork which is so widely used in making bottle stoppers. In the African villages, cork is put to many other uses such as for making sandals, and floats for fishing nets. It is even used to build houses as it keeps the home cool in summer."

"I didn't know that a single tree can be so full of gifts for us! I now know why my teacher said that the oak is really the king of trees."

"I have to agree with your teacher, Dana," said grandpa. "The oak tree is truly a wonderful gem in nature. In the old days, the charcoal was made from the oak branches. Charcoal when mixed with Sulphur and saltpetre becomes explosive gunpowder."

"And yet, I haven't told you one of the most important uses of oak," grandpa said mischievously. "Can you guess what it is?"

"Timber, dada," said Sidra smilingly.

When Daria and Dana looked astonished at her knowledge, Sidra explained how she had observed her uncle Aman, the farmhand making a boat from oak wood and that's how she knew about it.

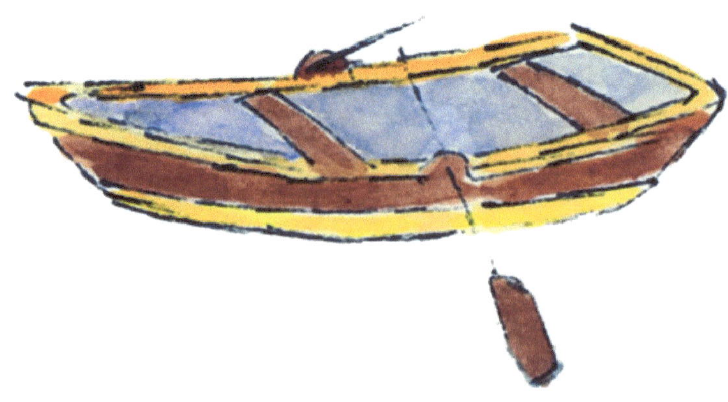

Her uncle had mentioned to Sidra that hardwoods such as oak are especially suitable for making the outer frame of boats.

"Yes, Sidra is right," agreed grandpa. "Timber or oak wood is used for many purposes such as building houses, furniture and axe handles. The wood used for shipbuilding comes from a special type of oak called, live oak, which grows in southern America. Its wood is very strong. I am afraid that live oak is getting scarcer and scarcer every day. An oak tree takes about a hundred years to fully grow, so if you cut a tree, a new oak tree would take long in coming."

Daria who was sitting in grandpa's lap had closed her eyes and was dreaming of a wonderful life in the tree house on top of the oak tree. Grandpa gathered Daria in his arms, and together they went in the house, with grandpa singing softly...

"...And I feel as if I were a baby too,
      When I hear that old song
      I have known so long...
Hush! my little one, go to sleep,
And mother will give you the moon to keep..."

oak bottle
stopper
oak
acorn
oak log
growth
rings
leaves from
different
types of
oak trees

"The Grapes are Sour," says Mr. Fox

Mr. Fox has a longing for grapes,
He jumps but the bunch still escapes.

It was late spring, and it was raining as usual. Dana and Daria couldn't go out to play. They sought out grandpa and entreated him for a story.

Grandpa agreed and said he would tell them a story about Mr. Fox who was a red fox. Dada began his story with some fun facts about the red fox which is one of the many species of foxes found in North America.

The red fox is a native of Canada and has a long-pointed face with a white chest and belly. Foxes depend on their eyesight, sense of smell and hearing to hunt. They can hear mice under snow, and smell rabbit nests hidden in long grass. They hunt small animals such as mice, squirrels, hares, and birds. They sometimes bring injured animals to their dens so their young kits can learn to kill. While the foxes are usually carnivorous, in summer when the fruits are ripening and insects come out of the ground, they will also eat birds' eggs and chicks, as well as insects, berries and fruits.

It was a beautiful summer evening and the beautiful red fox had been foraging all over the village. Last night, it had feasted on the frogs near the fishpond, but now Mr. Fox was hungry again. It searched everywhere for a rabbit to catch, or even the remains of chicken bones thrown by the housewives, but so far, its efforts had gone unrewarded.

Passing close to farmhouse, the fox spied a bunch of luscious purple grapes hanging on the tall trellis. The hungry red fox's mouth watered as it gazed longingly at the grapes which seemed ready to burst with juice. The fox thought, "I wouldn't mind dessert, as dinner is proving to be so elusive."

Unlike its cousin, the gray fox, the red fox was not an adept tree climber. Yet, the sight of the ripe and juicy grapes deepened the pangs of hunger and Mr. Fox bounded towards the trellis and sprang for the low hanging branch. Alas, it missed. Even as the branch swayed tantalizingly low, it proved to be out of reach.

Mr. Fox jumped again and again but failed to get a toehold on the branch.

Disappointed and tired, Mr. Fox slunk away, consoling itself, "These worthless grapes look so green and sour. I shall not bother anymore to grab this trash which is not even fit for pigs to eat."

Grandpa concluded the story with a smile. "My children, just like the red fox, many people pretend to disparage and dislike that which is not within their reach. We should work hard to achieve our goals instead of pretending that it is not worth the try."

The rain had stopped now. After thanking dada for his wonderful story, Dana ran out to join Sidra who was now outside floating her paper boat in the water puddles.

Daria who was very kindhearted wondered how it feels to be a hungry animal scavenging for food for its babies in a hostile world. She thoughtfully sat down by the window to make a sketch of the fox.

"Poor Mr. Fox," Daria whispered, "You are so graceful and gorgeous. I would have shared some of my dinner with you if I had realized how hungry you were."

Three Fishes

Dana and Daria were visiting Sidra, who lived with her uncle near the fishpond. Sidra's uncle Aman had prepared for them a tasty meal of fried fish with red onions, and roasted cauliflower.

Aman was especially proud of the giant onions that he had harvested recently. He had planted the onions in the fall just before the snow had started falling, and soon after the snow melted, the onions plants had started to mature. Dana was amazed to learn that even with the fields fully covered with snow, the plants had survived under the ground. The onions had become ready for harvesting towards the end of the spring and the kids collected some onions to take back to grandpa.

After lunch Aman brought over a pitcher of chilled linden tea infused with garden fresh mint leaves. As they sat in the cool shade of a giant maple tree, lazily sipping their drink, Aman asked, "Would you like me to tell you the story of the three fishes?" As the three kids eagerly nodded, Aman smiled and began his story.

Once upon a time, in the fishpond, there lived three fishes. The three fishes were good friends and yet they had very different character traits. One of the fishes was very intelligent, another fish was half-intelligent, and the third fish was foolish.

The small pond had greenery all around it and the foliage sheltered the fishes from intruders. The three fishes lived happily, and life was very peaceful, until one day came … a man carrying a net!

The intelligent fish watched the man through the water and realized he was a fisherman. She raced to alert her friends about this danger that lurked so close. The intelligent fish said to her friends, "Based on my experiences and the stories I have heard, the safest thing to do is to leave this pond immediately."

The other two fishes however disagreed with the intelligent fish as they didn't want to leave the comfort of their home. The intelligent fish, with a sad heart said goodbye to her friends and swam away to the safety of the ocean.

The half-intelligent fish felt a momentary pang of nervousness as her friend and guide, the intelligent fish, parted from them. She then thought, "I will hide inside the rotting buffalo carcass in the middle of the pond." Inside the smelly skeleton, the half-intelligent fish repented her decision of not leaving the pond with her friend and mentor, the intelligent fish.

The fisherman was disgusted by the malodorous buffalo body and stayed away from it, and the half-intelligent fish escaped being caught.

The half-intelligent fish through companionship of her friend and mentor, the wise fish, had learned to be quick-witted. Her resourcefulness saved her life.

The foolish fish, however, was completely at sea, now that none of her friends were around to counsel her. She agitatedly jumped about pretending to be clever but got trapped in the net.

As she sat uncomfortably on the terrible hot frying pan, the foolish fish understood that, bounded by her immediate perceptions, she had lacked farsightedness. Her friend and guide, the wise fish had realized that her true home is not the pond in which she had grown up, but the boundless ocean which she had never seen.

The wise fish suffers in her difficult quest for the infinite, but by putting in hard work, she achieves long lasting success.

As Aman concluded his story, Dana finished his painting as well, and folded up his watercolor box. Dana and Daria said goodbye to Sidra and her uncle and walked back to their farmhouse hand in hand.

It was a gorgeous afternoon. The day had been sunny and warm, but the breeze of the late afternoon was already blowing in from river, bringing freshness and life in the air. Watching the two kids coming up the garden path, grandpa felt glad that their farm visit had turned out to be so much fun.

The Light of the Heart

From Mevlana Jalal al-Din Muhammad Rumi's Masnavi

The light which gives light to the eye is the light of the heart,
The light which gives light to the heart is the Light of God,
And the Light of God is pure and sublime.

Goodbye for now...

You now come to the end of this book. We hope you enjoyed it. For other books in this series, and many other free and fun stories and drawings please visit **sagateller.com**

Thank You!

www.ingramcontent.com/pod-product-compliance
Lightning Source LLC
Chambersburg PA
CBHW040315240726
48664CB00006B/1498